TIGERS

TIGERS

JENNY MARKERT

THE CHILD'S WORLD

DESIGN
Bill Foster of Albarella & Associates, Inc.

PHOTO CREDITS
Leonard Rue III: front cover, back cover, 6, 30
Darryl W. Bush: 2, 8, 15
W. Perry Conway: 10, 13
Jeanne Drake: 16, 19, 21, 23, 24, 27
The Zoological Society of San Diego: 29

This book is a presentation of Newfield Publications, Inc.
For information about Newfield Publications book clubs for children
write to: **Newfield Publications, Inc.,**
4343 Equity Drive, Columbus, Ohio 43228.

Published by arrangement with The Child's World, Inc.
Newfield Publications is a federally registered
trademark of Newfield Publications, Inc.

1996 edition

Library of Congress Cataloging-in-Publication Data
Markert, Jenny
Tigers/by Jenny Markert
p. cm. — (Child's World Wildlife Library)
Summary: Describes the physical characteristics and behavior of the tiger
in its natural habitat.
ISBN 0-89565-722-8
1. Tigers — Juvenile literature.   [1. Tigers.]   I. Title.
II. Series.   91-13372
QL737.C23M3635 1991   CIP
599.74'428—dc20   AC

For Dad

Deep in the forests of Asia, animals come to life as the sun sinks toward the horizon. The temperature is dropping, and it's time to eat. Monkeys nibble tender leaves, birds search for insects, and deer sip water from a stream. Suddenly, a stirring tiger breaks the peaceful scene. As the tiger creeps through the trees, all the animals freeze and stare. Some screech messages of warning to the other animals. They know the tiger is on the prowl, and any one of them could be its next meal!

When you first see a tiger, you may think they all look alike. Indeed, most have orange coats with black stripes. However, if you look closely at the markings on tigers' faces, you will see lots of differences. Each tiger has a unique stripe pattern. One tiger, the white tiger, is easy to pick out. Unlike other tigers, it has white fur with brown stripes!

Along with lions, tigers are the biggest cats on earth. One kind of tiger, called the *Siberian*, is bigger than all other cats. From nose to tail a male Siberian tiger can grow to 12 feet long. He may weigh more than four full-grown men!

Wild tigers live only in Asia and surrounding islands. They are highly adaptable animals and can survive in many different habitats. Siberian tigers live in mountains where there is lots of snow. Other types of tigers live in grasslands, jungles, or marshes.

Tigers like to live by themselves. They live in groups only when they are raising their young. A single tiger lives in a small area called a *range*. This is where the tiger sleeps and hunts. A female tiger also raises her young on the range.

A tiger marks its range by scratching trees and urinating on bushes. This leaves a scent that other tigers can smell. When an intruding tiger detects the scent, it usually finds another place to live. Sometimes, however, an intruder will challenge the other tiger to a fight. The winner of the fight takes over the range. The loser must search for a new place to live.

When they are not patrolling their ranges, tigers are usually resting. They sleep much of the day. Unlike most other cats, tigers are not afraid of water. Adult tigers often rest in a cool stream or water hole. They even swim across lakes or rivers to find new places to live and hunt.

Tigers hunt only when it is cool outside, usually late in the afternoon or early at night. Tigers normally hunt alone, by ambush. A tiger begins a hunt by hiding in tall grass or bushes. Here, the tiger is nearly invisible. Its stripes blend in with the colors and shapes of the vegetation.

A tiger may wait for hours until an unsuspecting victim wanders nearby. When an animal comes close, the tiger creeps forward, keeping its body low to the ground. If the animal looks in its direction, the tiger freezes and stays perfectly still.

Finally, the tiger leaps out of the grass and races after the surprised animal. Once it catches up, the tiger swats the animal with its powerful front paw. Then the tiger uses its big front teeth to clamp onto the neck of its prey.

If a tiger kills an animal in an open area, it drags the meal into hiding. The tiger is very strong. It may carry a meal several miles before feeling safe enough to eat. Once secure, the tiger sits down and gorges itself. A tiger can eat 65 pounds of meat at one sitting. That's like eating 300 hot dogs!

After a meal, a tiger's belly is too full to move. The tiger sits down and cleans its fur like a house cat. Before dozing off for a nap, the tiger hides any meat that remains from the kill, covering it with grass, leaves, or tree branches. Later, when the tiger feels hungry again, it returns to eat the leftovers.

Tigers eat just about whatever they want, depending on where they live. Tigers that live in marshlands eat fish, frogs, crabs, and lizards. Forest-dwelling tigers eat monkeys and birds. Tigers that live on grassy plains prefer to hunt for wild boar and deer. They also kill elephants and rhinoceroses, but usually only the weak or young.

Tigers are not people-eaters by nature. In fact, tigers usually avoid people. If a healthy tiger attacks a human, it usually has a good reason. It may have been taken by surprise or may be defending its cubs.

Many animals are afraid of tigers because of their size and strength. However, when tigers are young, they themselves live in danger. Lions, crocodiles, and wild dogs steal tiger cubs from their mothers. If they are really hungry, other tigers will even eat young cubs.

When tigers are born, they drink their mother's milk. Within a few months, the cubs begin to eat meat that their mother brings to them. Soon after that, the cubs begin to watch their mother hunt. They eat the fresh kill with her. During the next two years, the mother tiger teaches her cubs how to catch their own food. Like any good teacher, the mother scolds her cubs if they misbehave. Once the young tigers can catch their own food, they leave their mother and search for their own ranges.

Unfortunately, much of the land that tigers used to roam is now used by people. Today, more tigers live in zoos than in the wild. At public zoos, people delight in the tiger's beauty, strength, and playfulness. However, behind a fenced cage, the tiger's fierce power and killing instincts are hard to appreciate. Animals in the wild are well aware of this threat. They watch carefully whenever a tiger is near.